A Pope of Surprises

The first five years
of Benedict XVI's Papacy

by Helena Scott and Ethel Tolansky

*All booklets are published thanks to the
generous support of the members of the
Catholic Truth Society*

CATHOLIC TRUTH SOCIETY
PUBLISHERS TO THE HOLY SEE

Contents

1. A Pope of Surprises 3

2. A call to love and dialogue
   First year: 2005 6

3. Opening new frontiers
   Second year: 2006 18

4. A call to see the true face of Jesus
   Third year: 2007 25

5. A voice for the ethical reasoning of humanity
   Fourth year: 2008 37

6. Foundations for the future
   Fifth year: 2009 46

7. Most intellectual of popes
   Sixth year: 2010 59

Bibliography 66

1

A Pope of Surprises

"A simple and humble labourer in the Lord's vineyard." This was how the newly elected Pope described himself on 19th April 2005.

In the five years since his election, Pope Benedict XVI has travelled all over the world, spoken to millions of people, and written in depth on a vast range of subjects. He has done everything within his power, not to make himself known, but to make God truly known and loved. And he has done all of this by being the person he is, not holding back from any opportunity to give himself through communication and hard work.

At the time of his election, plenty of people were ready to predict or guess what this new papacy would bring. It is fair to say that Pope Benedict has surprised everyone, accomplishing far more than was expected, and in very different ways from anything that could have been forecast.

Dialogue and love

He has proved his genuine love for everyone: Catholics, faithful and leaders of other Christian denominations, those of other religions or none. He has been proactive in establishing dialogue with them, showing that he understands and values the best in them. In this way, he has demonstrated that when he says that God loves everyone, this is not just words. He shows God's love for everyone by sharing it, in the way he loves everyone himself, and is open to all. This is shown in his deep, determined commitment to ecumenism.

No-one is outside his concern. Just one instance among many is his effort to guide and help the different elements of the Catholic Church in China, which is in a very complicated position. On 27th May 2007 he wrote a letter to Chinese Catholics setting out what the Church is, why she is not involved in politics, and who the Bishops are in the Church, to clarify Chinese Catholics' and state officials' understanding of these things and so enable them to move towards a solution of the problems they face. He proposed a World Day of Prayer for the Church in China, suggesting that: "the date 24 May could in the future become an occasion for the Catholics of the whole world to be united in prayer with the Church which is in China. This day is dedicated to the liturgical memorial of Our Lady, Help of Christians, who is venerated with great devotion at the Marian

Shrine of Sheshan in Shanghai. I would like that date to be kept as a day of prayer for the Church in China."

Theology and liturgy

The Pope's love for God is also shown in his love for the liturgy, which is the adoration and worship of God by the Church as a whole. Like all his predecessors, he has worked to enrich the liturgy and the theology that underlies it. He has explained that the liturgy is a living organism, an expression of the Church's life of prayer, and as such, development in the liturgy has to come about in a living, organic way, not as something artificially planned and imposed on it. Because the liturgy is the worship of the whole Church, it is not the property of any one individual, and therefore individual ideas of "creativity" or "self-expression" are misguided and out of place.

Sacred Scripture is also a permanent focus of the Pope's inner life and his teaching. "In the Church Fathers we find the notion that truth consists of a unity of diverse elements, much as a symphony brings into a single, harmonious whole the music played on a variety of instruments. This is how it is with the biblical theology of Benedict," says Scott Hahn in his book *The Biblical Theology of Benedict XVI* (p. 16).

2

A call to love and dialogue
First year: 2005

Catholics and Jews – a future of hope

Pope Benedict held his first audience for 25 Jewish leaders from Israel, the United States, Europe and Latin America on 9th June 2005. In his address to them, he said that "The history of relations between our two communities has been complex and often painful, but I am convinced that the spiritual patrimony treasured by Christians and Jews is itself the source of the wisdom and inspiration capable of guiding us toward a future of hope in accordance with the divine plan." He praised the Vatican II document *Nostra Aetate*, recalling that it urged greater understanding and esteem between Christians and Jews and that it "deplored all manifestations of hatred, persecution and anti-Semitism." He added: "At the very beginning of my pontificate, I wish to assure you that the Church remains firmly committed, in her catechesis and in every aspect of her life, to implementing this decisive teaching." The Pope said that for both Catholics and Jews, the painful past could not be forgotten. "Remembrance of the past remains for both communities a moral imperative and a source of purification in our efforts to pray and work for reconciliation, justice, respect for human dignity and for that peace which is ultimately a gift from the Lord himself." And he called for "continued reflection on the profound historical, moral and theological questions presented by the experience of the Holocaust."

Dear young people - WYD, Cologne

The very day after his election, Benedict XVI promised that he would fulfil a commitment made by John Paul II: to go to the World Youth Day in Cologne, Germany, from 18th to 21st August 2005. And in his homily at the Mass of his inauguration as Pope on 24th April 2005, he made a point of ending with a message to young people. "Dear young people: Do not be afraid of Christ! He takes nothing away, and he gives you everything. When we give ourselves to him, we receive a hundredfold in return. Yes, open, open wide the doors to Christ – and you will find true life."

When he arrived in Cologne, he took up the theme that had been announced for this Twentieth World Youth Day: "We have come to worship Him." He described the journey of the Magi in search of the new King as a geographical journey that was followed by a more important one: a spiritual journey to find how they could serve the cause of good – serve God – in truth and justice. The Pope then invited all young people to see how this applies to their own lives. We too, he said, have to set out and be prepared to change our ideas as we learn progressively more about who God is, in Jesus Christ, and what he wants of us.

He helped them to see and understand the "true face of the Church":

> The Church is like a human family, but at the same time it is also the great family of God, through which he establishes an overarching communion and unity that embraces every continent, culture and nation. So we are glad to belong to this great family that we see here; we are glad to have brothers and friends all over the world. Here in Cologne we discover the joy of belonging to a family as vast as the world, including Heaven and earth, the past, the present, the future and every part of the earth. In this great band of pilgrims we walk side by side with Christ, we walk with the star that enlightens our history.

He did not gloss over the other aspects of the Church. He touched on negative events in order to show how God could draw something positive out of them.

> There is much that could be criticized in the Church. We know this and the Lord himself told us so: it is a net with good fish and bad fish, a field with wheat and darnel. Pope John Paul II, as well as revealing the true face of the Church in the many saints that he canonized, also asked pardon for the wrong that was done in the course of history through the words and deeds of members of the Church. In this way he showed us our own true image and urged us to take our place, with all our faults and weaknesses, in the procession of the saints that began with the Magi from the East. It is actually consoling to realize that there is darnel in the Church. In this way, despite all our defects, we can still hope to be counted among the disciples of Jesus, who came to call sinners.

Example of the Saints

He offered them the example of the saints, especially four from the twentieth century – Maximilian Kolbe, Edith Stein, Mother Teresa of Calcutta and Padre Pio

– and pointed out that the Saints are the real reformers, since their radical demands are based on truth and love.

In the last century we experienced revolutions with a common programme – expecting nothing more from God, they assumed total responsibility for the cause of the world in order to change it. And this, as we saw, meant that a human and partial point of view was always taken as an absolute guiding principle. Absolutizing what is not absolute but relative is called totalitarianism. It does not liberate man, but takes away his dignity and enslaves him. It is not ideologies that save the world, but only a return to the living God, our Creator, the guarantor of our freedom, the guarantor of what is really good and true. True revolution consists in simply turning to God who is the measure of what is right and who at the same time is everlasting love. And what could ever save us apart from love?

At the Mass on the following day, the Pope spoke of the mystery of the Blessed Eucharist and helped the young people to understand why in the Eucharist, the Last Supper and the Crucifixion are all one:

By making the bread into his Body and the wine into his Blood, Jesus anticipates his death, he accepts it in his heart, and he transforms it into an action of love. What on the outside is simply brutal violence – the Crucifixion – from within becomes an act of total self-giving love.

Judaism and Christianity – the path of dialogue

As well as the gatherings for the World Youth Day itself, Pope Benedict took the opportunity to visit the Cologne Synagogue on 19th August and spoke to Jewish leaders. All his writings, from his earliest time as a teacher in Germany, show a profound knowledge, love, understanding and respect of the Old Testament as the Jewish scriptures. His theological reflections on the Bible are constantly enriched by his profound understanding of the Hebrew words and their implications. In Cologne, he raised the same themes as he had discussed in his meeting two months earlier with Jewish leaders from different countries, underlining the fact that *Nostra Aetate*

> recalls the common roots and the immensely rich spiritual heritage that Jews and Christians share. Both Jews and Christians recognize in Abraham their father in faith, and they look to the teachings of Moses and the prophets. Jewish

spirituality, like its Christian counterpart, draws nourishment from the Psalms. With St Paul, Christians are convinced that 'the gifts and the call of God are irrevocable' (Rom 11: 29). In considering the Jewish roots of Christianity, my venerable Predecessor John Paul II, quoting a statement by the German Bishops, affirmed that 'whoever meets Jesus Christ meets Judaism'.

Pope Benedict said that the dialogue between Judaism and Christianity, "if it is to be sincere, must not gloss over or underestimate the existing differences: in those areas in which, due to our profound convictions in faith, we diverge, and indeed, precisely in those areas, we need to show respect and love for one another."

The Ten Commandments, he said, are "a shared legacy and commitment. They are not a burden, but a signpost showing the path leading to a successful life. This is particularly the case for the young people whom I am meeting in these days and who are so dear to me. My wish is that they may be able to recognize in the Ten Commandments our common foundation, a 'lamp for their steps, a light for their path' (cf. Ps 119: 105)."

Muslims and Christians

He also met representatives of Muslim communities, at the Archbishop's residence in Cologne. Again his speech to them emphasized what the different religious communities have in common, encouraging them to work together to uproot hatred and rancour from people's hearts as the only way to defeat terrorism. He repeated what he had said a few months earlier in Rome: "the Church wants to continue building bridges of friendship with the followers of all religions, in order to seek the true good of every person and of society as a whole."

He paid special attention to future priests, meeting seminarians of the Cologne diocese and giving them a notable address about their vocation and the meaning of being a priest in the Church. Taking up the theme of the World Youth Day, and talking about the calling addressed to all by Christ, he said, "The seminarian experiences the beauty of that call in a moment of grace which could be defined as 'falling in love'. His soul is filled with amazement, which makes him ask in prayer: 'Lord, why me?' But love knows no 'why'; it is a free gift to which one responds with the gift of self."

In an address to the German Bishops, he detailed the challenges facing the Church not only in Germany but in Europe and worldwide, and highlighted three aspects in particular as the focus for the Bishops' work: catechesis, the pastoral care of vocations, and the pastoral care of the family.

Deus Caritas Est – God is Love: first encyclical

The Pope's first encyclical, *Deus Caritas Est* ("God is Love", 1 John 4: 8 and 16), was published on 25th December 2005. Its double theme is God as Love, and '*Caritas*', charity, as the practice of love in and by the Church. The encyclical was eagerly awaited as a manifesto of the work the Pope intended to undertake, and it surpassed people's expectations. It showed that all the Pope's work was the fruit of his prayer, his loving inner dialogue with God, that he did and wanted to do nothing except fulfil God's will to his utmost capacity. As he said, quoting Pope Gregory the Great in his *Pastoral Rule*, "the good pastor must be rooted in contemplation. Only in this way will he be able to take upon himself the needs of others and make them his own." By taking as his theme the love, charity, that originates in God's own being, the Pope invited, or challenged, people to return to that same source and to stop looking at the Church, the world or their own lives in merely earthbound terms. He looked at the different ways in which love is experienced and understood, culminating with:

> [the] love which involves a real discovery of the other, moving beyond the selfish character that prevailed earlier. Love now becomes concern and care for the other. No longer is it self-

seeking, a sinking in the intoxication of happiness; instead it seeks the good of the beloved: it becomes renunciation and it is ready, and even willing, for sacrifice.

The true nature of love

The encyclical is enormously rewarding to read. Starting from the nature of God's own love, the Pope explores the ways in which God loves us, how Jesus Christ is incarnate Love, how we love him, and how we love one another. He develops at length the meaning of love of neighbour as proclaimed by our Lord in the Gospels. Love of our neighbour, he says, "can only take place on the basis of an intimate encounter with God (...) Going beyond exterior experiences, I perceive in others an interior desire for a sign of love, of concern."

Having examined the true meaning of love, the Pope shows that what passes for love in this age – the "exaltation of the body", i.e. love reduced to only sex and selfishness – trivializes both sex and love. He replaces this notion with considerations of self-giving love as shown by Jesus' act of self-oblation. It is through the Eucharist which we share, that "we become 'one body', completely joined in a single existence. Love of God and love of neighbour are now truly united: God incarnate draws us all to himself" (no. 14).

The first part of the encyclical ends with a discussion of the double commandment of love: "No longer is it a question, then, of a 'commandment' imposed from without and calling for the impossible, but rather of a freely-bestowed experience of love from within, a love which by its very nature must then be shared with others."

True nature of charity

In the second part, he shows why charitable activity is always an essential part of the work of the Church, and what is distinctive about the Church's social and charitable outreach at every level – parochial, diocesan, national and international. "Love, *caritas*, will always prove necessary, even in the most just society. There is no ordering of the state so just that it can eliminate the need for a service of love." And he goes on,

> We are dealing with human beings, and human beings always need something more than technically proper care. They need humanity. They need heartfelt concern. Those who work for the Church's charitable organizations must be distinguished by the fact that they do not

merely meet the needs of the moment, but they dedicate themselves to others with heartfelt concern, enabling them to experience the richness of their humanity. Consequently, in addition to their necessary professional training, these charity workers need a "formation of the heart": they need to be led to that encounter with God in Christ which awakens their love and opens their spirits to others.

This leads to a re-affirmation of the point made at the end of the first part: "As a result, love of neighbour will no longer be for them a commandment imposed, so to speak, from without, but a consequence deriving from their faith, a faith which becomes active through love."

3

Opening new frontiers
Second year: 2006

Visiting Poland - the land of John Paul II

Pope Benedict XVI made a pilgrimage to Poland, from 25th to 28th May 2006. He visited Warsaw, Czestochowa, Krakow, and on 27th May made a special visit to Lagniewniki, the birthplace of the devotion to Divine Mercy spread by St Faustina Kowalska. Here he had a meeting with the sick, to whom he gave a very short address, explaining that

> on this occasion we encounter two mysteries: the mystery of human suffering and the mystery of Divine Mercy. At first sight these two mysteries seem to be opposed to one another. But when we study them more deeply in the light of faith, we find that they are placed in reciprocal harmony through the mystery of the Cross of Christ.

This was a theme he was to take up and explore further in his annual Messages for the World Day of the Sick, on 11th February, the feast of Our Lady of Lourdes.

He celebrated an open-air Mass in Blonie Park in Krakow, a huge space which was still not large enough for the number of people who came, totalling around a million. In his homily, he spoke of the Gospel of the Ascension of the Lord, and said,

> At the beginning of the second year of my Pontificate, I have felt a deep need to visit Poland and Krakow as a pilgrim in the footsteps of my predecessor. I wanted to breathe the air of his homeland. I wanted to see the land where he was born, where he grew up and undertook his tireless service to Christ and the universal Church. I wanted especially to meet the living men and women of his country, to experience your faith, which gave him life and strength, and to know that you continue firm in that faith. Here I wish to ask God to preserve that legacy of faith, hope and charity which John Paul II gave to the world, and to you in particular.

He ended with a heartfelt appeal to the congregation:

> I ask you, finally, to share with the other peoples of Europe and the world the treasure of your faith, not least as a way of honouring the

memory of your countryman, who, as the Successor of Saint Peter, did this with extraordinary power and effectiveness. And remember me in your prayers and sacrifices, even as you remembered my great Predecessor, so that I can carry out the mission Christ has given me. I ask you to stand firm in your faith! Stand firm in your hope! Stand firm in your love! Amen!

The Shoah – learning from the past

From Krakow Pope Benedict went to the site of the World War II concentration camp at Oswiecim or Auschwitz, where he gave a moving address that was really a cry to God and a prayer for reconciliation. It was an extraordinary moment: the German Pope at the site where German Nazis had murdered around a million people, mostly Jews and Poles. In deference to Polish sensitivities he spoke in Italian for most of this trip, as well as Polish for shorter greetings and prayers. But here in Auschwitz he also spoke his native German, so that he should not appear to be shying away from the reality of the situation. Among other things, he pointed out that "The past is never simply the past. It always has something to say to us; it tells us the paths to take and the paths not to take." As those present on this occasion will always recall, a heavy thunderstorm gave way to a brilliant rainbow as the Pope concluded his address.

He also went to Wadowice, where Pope John Paul II was born and grew up, and recalled the importance that the church there played in the life of his "great predecessor".

Centrality of families - World Meeting, Valencia

Another pastoral visit was to the Fifth World Meeting of Families held in Valencia, Spain, from 8th to 9th July 2006, where he taught the faithful that "None of us gave ourselves life or singlehandedly learned how to live. All of us received from others both life itself and its basic truths, and we have been called to attain perfection in relationship and loving communion with others." He underlined the indissolubility of marriage, "the setting where men and women are enabled to be born with dignity, and to grow and develop in an integral manner."

Faith, reason and Islam - Regensburg

In September 2006 Pope Benedict visited Germany once again. As well as ceremonies at Munich and the shrine of Our Lady at Altotting, he visited his old university of Regensburg (Ratisbon) on 12th September and gave an address on the place of reason in understanding and defending the faith, explaining why, if the Word of God is indeed reason, violence cannot be rationalized as part of religion. In the course of this, he quoted an ancient dialogue between a Byzantine Emperor and a Muslim on whether violence can be used to impose faith. The Emperor explains that "Violence is incompatible with the nature of God and the nature of the soul. 'God', he says, 'is not pleased by blood – and not acting reasonably is contrary to God's nature. Faith is born of the soul, not the body. Whoever would lead someone to faith needs the ability to speak well and to reason properly, without violence and threats... To convince a reasonable soul, one does not need a strong arm, or weapons of any kind, or any other means of threatening a person with death...'." Because the Emperor referred to Mohammed, many Muslims who had not read the full text of the Pope's speech took violent offence at the reference. In fact, the Pope makes it clear that the Emperor "addresses his interlocutor with a startling brusqueness, a brusqueness that we find unacceptable."

The Pope showed his concern that Islam has never really grasped the fundamental importance of the relationship between faith and reason. He did so in the hopes that it might encourage Islamic thinkers to consider the place of reason in any coherent worldview. He does not, however, make the mistake of imagining that Western liberalist modes of thought, or political systems, can or should be imposed onto Islamic traditions in an effort to turn them into Western-style democracies. He understands democracy as being essentially the product of Christianity, without which it is quickly undermined.

Peace through dialogue – visit to Turkey

Following this journey Pope Benedict made a three-day visit to Turkey, from 28th November to 1st December 2006. Speaking to journalists on the way there, he set out his aims for the trip. Acknowledging that a three-day pastoral visit was not going to produce any sudden change in current situations, he said that he hoped nevertheless to establish a fraternal exchange with the Orthodox churches represented there, and to instigate a dialogue of reason and respect with the Muslim community. The visit could only be symbolic, but the symbol was, he hoped, "rich in reality". On his arrival, Pope Benedict was welcomed by Turkish Prime Minister Recep Tayyip Erdogan. He met members of the Diplomatic Corps, and spoke about true peace and the way to achieve it in the international community. He underlined the need for sincere dialogue in achieving lasting peace. In Ankara, he greeted the Turkish

President Ahmet Necdet Sezer, who had invited him to the country, and made a visit to the Ataturk Mausoleum. On succeeding days he visited a shrine of Our Lady in Ephesus, and prayed with His Holiness the Orthodox Patriarch Bartholomew I and with His Beatitude Mesrob II Mutafyan, Armenian Patriarch, continuing the ecumenical dialogue and expressing his earnest desire for full loving union between the Catholic and Orthodox Churches.

His love of Scripture and the Apostles

Like his predecessors, Pope Benedict used the general audiences every Wednesday to help his hearers deepen their understanding of and love for the Church. Starting in 2005 with a series of discourses on the Psalms, as well as some of the Letters of St Paul, he devoted many of those in 2006 to a study of the individual Apostles, including St Paul again. He helped his hearers to understand the riches of their own heritage as members of the Church, to develop their devotion to the saints, to explore the teachings of the earliest years of the Church's life, and the treasure of the Scriptures.

4

A call to see the true face of Jesus
Third year: 2007

Sacramentum Caritatis - Eucharist as the Sacrament of Love

Pope John Paul II had written *Ecclesia de Eucharistia* in 2003, and the year when Pope John Paul II died and Pope Benedict XVI was elected had been celebrated in the whole Church as a Year of the Eucharist. It concluded in September 2005 with a Synod of Bishops about the Blessed Eucharist. Now, on 22nd February 2007, the Holy Father completed and signed *Sacramentum Caritatis*, his post-synodal Apostolic Exhortation on the Eucharist as the source and summit of the Church's life and mission. In an extended meditation on the Real Presence of our Lord in the Blessed Sacrament, the Pope explained that the Eucharist is the perfect heart of the liturgy, and that, since God is beauty, beauty has to be at the heart of the liturgy. "Like the rest of Christian revelation, the liturgy is inherently linked to beauty: it is *veritatis splendor* ('the radiance of Truth'). The liturgy is a radiant expression of the Paschal mystery, in which

Christ draws us to himself and calls us to communion. As St Bonaventure would say, in Jesus we contemplate beauty and splendour at their source" (no. 35).

Among many other aspects, the Pope looked at the Eucharist and priestly spirituality. The priest "is called to seek God tirelessly, while remaining attuned to the concerns of his brothers and sisters. An intense spiritual life will enable him to enter more deeply into communion with the Lord and to let himself be possessed by God's love, bearing witness to that love at all times, even the darkest and most difficult… If celebrated in a faith-filled and attentive way, Mass is formative in the deepest sense of the word, since it fosters the priest's configuration to Christ and strengthens him in his vocation" (no. 80). He spoke of the Eucharist and moral transformation (no. 82), quoting Pope John Paul II's encyclical *Veritatis Splendor*: "by sharing in the sacrifice of the Cross, the Christian partakes of Christ's self-giving love and is equipped and committed to live this same charity in all his thoughts and deeds." Pope Benedict continued,

> This appeal to the moral value of spiritual worship should not be interpreted in a merely moralistic way. It is before all else the joy-filled discovery of love at work in the hearts of those who accept the Lord's gift, abandon themselves to him and thus find true freedom. The moral

transformation implicit in the new worship instituted by Christ is a heartfelt yearning to respond to the Lord's love with one's whole being, while remaining ever conscious of one's own weakness... The moral urgency born of welcoming Jesus into our lives is the fruit of gratitude for having experienced the Lord's unmerited closeness.

The section on the Eucharist and mission (no. 84) took this idea a step further still:

In my homily at the Eucharistic celebration solemnly inaugurating my Petrine ministry, I said that "there is nothing more beautiful than to be surprised by the Gospel, by the encounter with Christ. There is nothing more beautiful than to know him and to speak to others of our friendship with him." These words are all the more significant if we think of the mystery of the Eucharist. The love that we celebrate in the Sacrament is not something we can keep to ourselves. By its very nature it demands to be shared with all. What the world needs is God's love; it needs to encounter Christ and to believe in him. The Eucharist is thus the source and summit not only of the Church's life, but also of her mission.

Church is always missionary - Brazil

Pope Benedict journeyed to Brazil from 9th to 14th May, 2007. The occasion was the Fifth General Conference of the Bishops of Latin America and the Caribbean. However, he made sure that his journey also included meetings with the disadvantaged and with young people. On his way to Brazil he referred to the expansion of Protestant sects there, saying that "The success of the sects shows, on the one hand, that there is a widespread thirst for God, a thirst for religion, that people want to be close to God and seek contact with him. On the other hand, of course, they accept those who present themselves and promise solutions to their problems of daily life. As the Catholic Church, we must implement the precise goal of the Fifth Conference, which is, we must be more missionary and therefore more dynamic in offering responses to the thirst for God, knowing that people, and the poor themselves, want God close to them."

Love for the poor and disadvantaged

On 12th May he visited a community for the rehabilitation of drug addicts, the Fazenda da Esperança, Guaratinguetá. He spoke words of love and hope to those undergoing rehabilitation, and those helping them. Throughout his pilgrimage his primary concern was to give a message of hope and rekindle love for and confidence in Jesus Christ as Saviour. In his homily at the canonization of Brother Antonio Galvao, the first Brazilian-born Saint, as well as following the life-story of the new Saint, he responded to the superficial attraction of non-Catholic sects by setting out once again the truth and beauty of the Catholic faith, and outlined what the Catholic Church is and does.

Summorum Pontificum - Extraordinary form of the Mass

Pope Benedict's "Motu Proprio *Summorum Pontificum*, on the use of the Roman Liturgy prior to the reform of 1970" was published on 7th July 2007. In it he opened up to priests and people the possibilities of celebrating and attending Mass in the older form of the Roman Rite, now referred to as the "Extraordinary Form". This was a long-awaited development which the Pope handled with his characteristic gentleness and understanding, and an appeal that this move would be an occasion for strengthening unity in the Church.

Pilgrimage to Austria

Benedict XVI made a visit to Austria from 7th to 9th September 2007, to take part in the celebrations of the 850th anniversary of the shrine of Our Lady,

Mariazell. He again emphasized that this was a pilgrimage, and expressed his desire to confirm Christians in the faith. Although time did not permit meetings with representatives of other religions, he wished to include a brief prayer before the monument to the Holocaust in Vienna, to express once again his solidarity and hopes for dialogue with "our Jewish brothers and sisters".

Spe Salvi – Saved in Hope: second encyclical

The Pope's second encyclical, *Spe Salvi* ("Saved in Hope", Romans 8:24) was published on 30th November 2007.

In it, with his usual depth of understanding and talent for teaching, the Pope reflected on just what Christian hope is and what it is not; what the grounds for Christian hope are; and then looked at what exactly we can hope for, given the current state of the world and the human condition. In order to do this, he built on the foundation laid in his first encyclical, *Deus Caritas Est*.

> It is not science that redeems man: man is redeemed by love. This applies even in terms of this present world. When someone has the experience of a great love in his life, this is a moment of "redemption" which gives a new meaning to his life. But soon he will also realize

that the love bestowed upon him cannot by itself resolve the question of his life. It is a love that remains fragile. It can be destroyed by death. The human being needs unconditional love. (...) If this absolute love exists, with its absolute certainty, then – only then – is man "redeemed", whatever should happen to him in his particular circumstances. This is what it means to say: Jesus Christ has "redeemed" us. Through him we have become certain of God, a God who is not a remote "first cause" of the world, because his only-begotten Son has become man, and of him everyone can say: "I live by faith in the Son of God, who loved me and gave himself for me" (Gal 2:20). (no. 26)

Responding to a crisis of faith

As he had done with love in *Deus Caritas Est*, the Holy Father opened up new ways of looking at hope. To come to know the true God is to receive hope. However, in the last centuries the meaning of hope has been watered down. This has brought about the present-day crisis of faith, which is essentially a crisis of Christian hope. The Holy Father traced the roots of this crisis of faith and hope in the common notion of progress in both science and politics. He warned about mistaken ideas of reason and freedom within belief in progress.

> Two categories become increasingly central to the idea of progress: reason and freedom. Progress is primarily associated with the growing dominion of reason, and this reason is obviously considered to be a force of good and a force for good. Progress is the overcoming of all forms of dependency – it is progress towards perfect freedom. Likewise freedom is seen purely as a promise, in which man becomes more and more fully himself. In both concepts – freedom and reason – there is a political aspect. The kingdom of reason, in fact, is expected as the new condition of the human race. (...) The two concepts of "reason" and "freedom", however, were tacitly interpreted as being in conflict with the shackles of faith and of the Church. (No. 18)

It is against this scenario that the Holy Father shows the persistence of Christian hope, giving a rapid sketch of the development of humanist and atheistic thought in the West through the centuries. The experiences of the French Revolution and Marxism offer Christians the opportunity to re-examine the concept of hope. "Christians (...) must learn anew in what their hope truly consists, what they have to offer to the world and what they cannot offer" (no. 22). So the present situation becomes a process of learning: "Flowing into this self-critique of the modern age there also has to be a self-critique of modern Christianity which must constantly renew its self-understanding, setting out from its roots." He shows the "ambiguity of progress": it is not all that it sets out to be, because not only does it have "new possibilities for good, but it also opens up appalling possibilities for evil" – what he calls "progress in the wrong hands." Freedom and reason can never be total, because of man's nature. The Pope's conclusion is that "reason therefore needs faith (...) reason and faith need one another in order to fulfil their true nature and their mission." Furthermore, "Freedom must constantly be won over for the cause of good."

A firm hope in God

What has remained through all the changes and turmoil in action and thought? "Man's great, true hope which holds firm in spite of all disappointments, can only be God" (no. 27). This love of God is not selfish, but opens up towards others, for "love of God is revealed in responsibility for others." In summarizing the journey of hope in the modern age, the Holy Father has demonstrated that Biblical hope has been "displaced by hope in the kingdom of man. (...) In the course of time, however, it has become clear that this hope is constantly receding." It does not really match up to man's aspirations. "It becomes evident that man has need of a hope that goes further. It becomes clear that only something infinite will suffice for him. (...) This great hope can only be God" (nos. 29-31).

The Pope helps readers see how to practise hope as a stable virtue through the school of prayer and suffering, referring to the book *Prayers of Hope* by the late Cardinal Nguyen Van Thuan. The last section of the encyclical is a long, impassioned prayer addressed to Mary, the Mother of God and "Star of Hope".

Jesus of Nazareth – a personal search

2007 also saw the publication of the Pope's book *Jesus of Nazareth*. It was to be the first of two books, covering the life of our Lord from the Baptism in the Jordan at the start of his public ministry, up to the Transfiguration. Pointing to the absurdity of a supposed distinction between the "historical Jesus" and the "Christ of faith", the Pope works to find "the true face of Jesus" who brought God to the world. He explains why the reconstructions of Jesus proposed by some Biblical scholars have been ultimately unsuccessful. "If you read a number of these reconstructions one after another, you see at once that far from uncovering an icon that has become obscured over time, they are much more like photographs of their authors and the ideals they hold."

The basis of his "personal search for the face of the Lord" is that "I see Jesus in light of his communion with the Father." He starts and ends with the Gospels: "I believe that this Jesus – the Jesus of the Gospels – is a historically plausible and convincing figure." The reason for concentrating on our Lord's public ministry is that "it struck me as the most urgent priority to present the figure and the message of Jesus in his public ministry, and so to help foster the growth of a living relationship with him."

It is not possible to give a reasonable summary of the whole book in this short account. The Pope brings his enormous knowledge of Biblical theology to bear on the subject, and sheds light on the Gospel accounts of Jesus by explaining the Old Testament and Jewish background of our Lord's words and actions, showing how Jesus brought the Old Testament to fulfilment in himself. He refers to Jacob Neusner's book, *A Rabbi Talks with Jesus* published in 2000, to show the way Jesus appeared to his contemporaries and to devout, open-minded Jewish believers today.

Among many guiding themes, the Pope develops the idea of heaven as the will of God: "Heaven is essentially the place where God's will is perfectly fulfilled" (p. 23) ... "Jesus himself is 'heaven' in the deepest and truest sense of the word – he in whom God's will is wholly done" (p. 150). The chapters cover the Baptism of Jesus, his temptations in the desert, his proclamation of the Kingdom of God, the Sermon on the Mount, the Beatitudes; the Torah of the Messiah; the Our Father; the Disciples; Jesus' parables, images used in the Gospel of St John, the Confession of St Peter's faith, and the Transfiguration, to conclude with Jesus' declaration of his own identity.

The Early Christians and the Fathers of the Church

Throughout the year 2007, Pope Benedict devoted his Wednesday general audiences to a study of the notable figures among the Early Christians, going on to the Fathers of the Church. In 2008 he would spend five of them on a detailed account of the life, work and thought of St Augustine, whose teachings had always been central to his own theological development.

5

A voice for the ethical reasoning of humanity
Fourth year: 2008

The Pope and the University - La Sapienza, Rome

On 17th January 2008 the Holy Father had been invited to give an address at the University of La Sapienza in Rome, at a ceremony marking the start of its academic year. However, a group of members of the University agitated against his visit, on the alleged grounds that in 1990 the then Cardinal Joseph Ratzinger had described the 17th-century Church trial against Galileo as "rational and just". (Those in favour of the papal visit pointed out that Cardinal Ratzinger had been quoting the Austrian-born philosopher Paul Feyerabend on Galileo, and had not said he agreed with the statement.) Rather than provoke conflict, the Pope, with his customary humility and patience, decided to cancel the visit. This caused great disappointment among the majority of the staff and students of La Sapienza, as well as to himself, since he had been looking forward, as always, to this meeting with an academic community.

The address he had written was read out at the ceremony, and greeted with enthusiastic cheering. Interestingly enough, it was a precise, carefully reasoned discussion of the nature and mission of the Papacy and the nature and mission of a University, and on that basis, of what a Pope can have to say to a University.

Voice of ethical reasoning

Benedict explained why "the Pope, in his capacity as Shepherd of his community, is also increasingly becoming a voice for the ethical reasoning of humanity"; and went on to pose the question of whether a Pope, whose judgements are based on faith, could have anything to say to people who do not share his faith. This leads to the question: "What is reason? How can one demonstrate that an assertion – especially a moral norm – is reasonable?" The Pope explained that the reason of religion cannot simply be dismissed by those who maintain a rigidly secularized rationality. This is partly because religious teachings derive from a responsible and well-thought-out tradition, which has developed satisfactory arguments to support them, and these arguments have stood the test of time. Down through the centuries, experience and demonstration – the historical source of human wisdom – are also a sign of the reasonableness and lasting significance of religious teachings. The Pope then showed that from the earliest centuries, Christian faith and teachings had not been received as a solid block to be fought for without understanding, nor as a sort of wish-fulfilment, but as "dispelling the mist of mythological religions in order to make way for the discovery of the God who is creative Reason, God who is Reason-Love".

The Church in America

In April 2008 Pope Benedict travelled to the United States. On the flight there, a journalist raised the question of the sex abuse of children by Catholic priests and the suffering this was causing the Church in America. The Holy Father spoke with great pain about how hard it was "to understand how it was possible for priests to fail in this way in the mission to give healing, to give God's love to these children. I am ashamed and we will do everything possible to ensure that this does not happen in future." He outlined the specific directions these efforts would take.

In America he visited Washington, meeting President Bush at the White House, and the Bishops of the United States at the National Shrine of the Immaculate Conception on 16th April, his birthday. He celebrated Mass at the Washington Nationals Stadium on 17th April, and then met representatives of other religions at the John Paul II Cultural Center. He gave a general address and then had a special exchange with representatives of the Jewish Community in the US.

Science and ethics must work together - UN

He went to New York, where he addressed the United Nations Assembly on 18th April. He spoke about the effects of globalization on Third World countries; reminded them of the need to protect the identity of the human person and the family in the context of scientific research and technological advances; and pointed out that "international action to preserve the environment and to protect various forms of life on earth must not only guarantee a rational use of technology and science, but must also rediscover the authentic image of creation. This never requires a choice to be made between science and ethics: rather it is a question of adopting a scientific method that is truly respectful of ethical imperatives." His major focus was on true human rights, in the context of the Universal Declaration of Human Rights whose sixtieth anniversary was then being celebrated.

On Saturday 19th April, the anniversary of his election, he celebrated Holy Mass with priests, men and women religious in St Patrick's Cathedral in New York, and afterwards met young people and seminarians, giving special attention to young people with disabilities. The following day he prayed at "Ground Zero" and celebrated Holy Mass at New York's Yankee Stadium. At every stage he gave greetings, addresses, homilies or speeches, taking every opportunity to open his hearers' eyes to the riches of Christ and the teachings of the Church.

One of the people who met him during his US journey described him as a "kindly-looking old man arrayed in various vesture of brilliant white, his countenance telling of such deep-seated joy in Christ and love of His Church, such that not even the most gifted artist could capture it."

Year of St Paul

To mark the two thousandth centenary of the birth of St Paul, the Holy Father proclaimed a "Year of St Paul" to be celebrated by the whole Church from 29th June 2008 to 29th June 2009 (the feast of Sts Peter and Paul). In his Wednesday audiences he returned to the figure, history, letters and message of St Paul, giving another twenty discourses about him from July 2008 to February 2009.

Be ambassadors of hope - WYD, Sydney

Pope Benedict went to the 23rd World Youth Day in Sydney, Australia from 12th to 21st July 2008. Here, after spending four days resting in "private time", he met representatives of other Christian denominations and other religions, and celebrated Mass for Australian Bishops, seminarians and novices. He had a special meeting with disadvantaged young people, and, having described the ways in which material possessions, possessive love, and power could be used as "false gods" that only bring death, he outlined the story of the prodigal son and went on, "Many of you must have had personal experience of what that young man went through." They had already taken wrong paths and then turned back onto "the path of life", he said, and he saluted their courage. He added, "Dear friends, I see you as ambassadors of hope to others in similar situations. You can convince them of the need to choose the path of life and shun the path of death, because you speak from experience. All through the Gospels, it was those who had taken wrong turnings who were particularly loved by Jesus, because once they recognized their mistake, they were all the more open to his healing message."

Don't be afraid to stand up for Christ

At the Mass of the World Youth Day itself, taking the WYD theme "You will receive power when the Holy Spirit comes upon you", the Holy Father spoke about the Sacrament of Confirmation which was to be celebrated as part of the Mass. "In this great assembly of young Christians from all over the world, we have had a vivid experience of the Spirit's presence and power in the life of the Church. We have seen the Church for what she truly is: the Body of Christ, a living community of love, embracing people of every race, nation and tongue, of every time and place, in the unity born of our faith in the Risen Lord." He went on, "What does it mean to receive the 'seal' of the Holy Spirit? It means being indelibly marked, inalterably changed, a new creation. For those who have received this gift, nothing can ever be the same! ... Being 'sealed with the Spirit' means not being afraid to stand up for Christ, letting the truth of the Gospel permeate the way we see, think and act, as we work for the triumph of the civilization of love."

Lourdes and the sick

For the celebrations of the 150th anniversary of the apparition of Our Lady at Lourdes, Pope Benedict visited France from 12th to 15th September 2008. During the visit, he met representatives from the world of culture at the Collège des Bernadins, Paris, and many other groups of people starting with the French Bishops and including, as always, young people and the sick. At Lourdes he celebrated Mass and gave a meditation for the Blessed Sacrament Procession. In the Eucharistic Celebration for the Sick, he spoke above all about Our Lady's smile as Bernadette had seen it at Lourdes, and said that "Without the Lord's help, the yoke of sickness and suffering weighs down on us cruelly. By receiving the Sacrament of the Sick, we seek to carry no other yoke than that of Christ, strengthened through his promise to us that his yoke will be easy to carry and his burden light (cf. Mt 11:30)."

The Benedict XVI Foundation

That same autumn saw the launch of "The Ratzinger Foundation", also known as "The Benedict XVI Foundation". Its purpose is to offer scholarships in theology to aspiring students who would not otherwise be able to afford further studies. The scholarships are funded by the sales of the Pope's published writings. The board of trustees, whose members include former students from Germany, Portugal, Ireland, Benin, and the United States, reflects the international scope of the foundation's outreach.

Blessed John Duns Scotus

On 28th October 2008 the Holy Father published a brief Apostolic Letter commemorating the seventh centenary of the death of Blessed John Duns Scotus, the Scottish theologian who died on 8th November 1308 and whose relics are honoured in Cologne, Germany. The Pope quoted appreciatively from Duns Scotus's writings on the Passion of our Lord and the Blessed Eucharist. He recalled how, among other titles, Duns Scotus was given that of *"doctor marianus"* for his writings on our Blessed Lady, especially on her Immaculate Conception. The Holy Father said, "we desire to remind scholars and everyone, believers and non-believers alike, of the path and method that Scotus followed in order to establish harmony between faith and reason, defining in this manner the nature of theology in order constantly to exalt action, influence, practice and love rather than pure speculation; in fulfilling this task he let himself be guided by the Magisterium of the Church and by a sound critical sense regarding growth in knowledge of the truth and was convinced that knowledge is valuable to the extent that it is applied in praxis."

6

Foundations for the future
Fifth year: 2009

The "Society of St Pius X" – offering reconcilliation

The "Society of St Pius X", founded in Switzerland in 1970 by the French Archbishop Marcel Lefebvre, rejected all the changes in the Roman Catholic Church, especially the liturgy, since the Second Vatican Council. On 21st January 2009, the Pope announced the lifting of the excommunication from the four bishops of the "Society of St Pius X" who had been ordained illicitly (without Papal approval) by the late Archbishop Lefebvre in 1988. This gesture was intended to pave the way for them, and other members of the Society, to return to full faithfulness to the Church.

Unfortunately, and through no fault of the Pope's, his gesture of reconciliation was seized upon by the media, who discovered that one of the four bishops was also a Holocaust denier. In the press in many countries, this was presented as though the Holy Father was endorsing such views, even though the memory of the Pope's visits to Auschwitz and the

Cologne Synagogue, and the things he said in his meetings with Jewish leaders on many occasions, ought to have been sufficient to dispel this idea. Patiently and humbly, the Pope set about rectifying and clarifying the situation, writing an open letter to all the Bishops in communion with Rome, and restoring communications with Jewish communities, which had been threatened by the uproar.

Cameroon and Angola – the Church and Aids

A very significant pastoral visit was the one he made to Cameroon and Angola, from 17th to 23rd March 2009. This aroused worldwide interest, which in the media mainly focused on his approach to the problem of Aids in Africa. In response to a question during the journey to Cameroon, he said, "I would say that this problem of Aids cannot be overcome merely with money, necessary though it is. If there is no human dimension, if Africans do not help [by responsible behaviour], the problem cannot be overcome by the distribution of prophylactics: on the contrary, they increase it. The solution must have two elements: firstly, bringing out the human dimension of sexuality, that is to say a spiritual and human renewal that would bring with it a new way of behaving towards others, and secondly, true friendship offered above all to those who are suffering, a willingness to make sacrifices and to practise self-denial, to be alongside the suffering... The Church does this, thereby offering an enormous and important contribution."

Hope to the sick and war weary

In Cameroon, once again, the Pope had meetings with the local Bishops, representatives of Muslim communities, and the sick. Here he spoke of Christ's "fraternal tenderness and benevolence towards all the broken-hearted, all whose bodies are wounded." He reminded his hearers that the person who helped Jesus in his final suffering by carrying the Cross with him was an African, Simon of Cyrene. "I pray, dear brothers and sisters, that you will be able to recognize yourselves in Simon of Cyrene. I pray, dear brothers and sisters who are sick, that many of you will encounter a Simon at your bedside." He spoke of our Lady at the foot of the Cross, and of St Joseph, quoting St Teresa of Avila's words about him, and concluding, "Saint Teresa saw in Saint Joseph not only an intercessor for bodily health, but also an intercessor for the health of the soul, a teacher of prayer." In Angola, at a meeting with young people, he recalled that Pope John Paul II had also met young people at the same place in 1992, and said "Today another Pope stands before you: with a different appearance, but with the same love in his heart, and he embraces all of you in Jesus Christ." He encouraged them to look to God with hope: "Yes, my friends! God makes all the difference... and more! God changes us; he makes us new!... He can walk with us as a friend in the present, carrying in his hand the book of our days."

Jordan and Israel – pilgrimage to Holy Land

From 8th to 15th May 2009 Pope Benedict XVI visited the Holy Land, starting at Amman, Jordan. He described his journey as a pilgrimage, and said that "I shall seek to contribute to peace not as an individual but in the name of the Catholic Church, and of the Holy See. We are not a political power, but a spiritual force, and this spiritual force is a reality that can contribute to advances in the peace process." The Church can do this, he said, through the power of prayer, through the correct formation of consciences, and through the power of reason. Referring to the difficulties and opportunities of inter-religious dialogue between the three Abrahamic religions, he explained that "it is important on the one hand to have bilateral dialogues – with the Jews and with Islam – and then also trilateral dialogue." He spoke with hope about the various developments, especially in the educational sphere, where young people from different cultures and religions were going to be able to study together.

Dialogue always built on mutual trust

In Israel, he went first to Jerusalem, then to Bethlehem, Nazareth, and back to Jerusalem. He met men and women religious, the Diplomatic Corps, and had ecumenical meetings with Orthodox and Anglican representatives. He visited the memorial for Jews killed in the Holocaust, Yad Vashem, where he reminded his hearers that "One can rob a neighbour of possessions, opportunity or freedom. One can weave an insidious web of lies to convince others that certain groups are undeserving of respect. Yet, try as one might, one can never take away the name of a fellow human being." At the refugee camp for Palestinians in Bethlehem, on Wednesday 13th May, the Pope spoke clearly of the conditions of the refugees and the general feeling of frustration they suffered. Underlining his constant theme of the need for dialogue, he said, "History has shown that peace can only come when the parties to a conflict are willing to move beyond their grievances and work together towards common goals, each taking seriously the concerns and fears of the other, striving to build an atmosphere of trust." At the Western Wall in Jerusalem he made a short, heartfelt prayer for peace.

Year for Priests

The Pope declared a Year for Priests marking the 150th anniversary of the death of St John Marie Vianney, 19th June 2009 to 11th June 2010 (feasts of the Sacred Heart of Jesus), with the motto "Faithfulness of Christ, Faithfulness of Priests". St John Marie Vianney was to be proclaimed Patron Saint of all priests in 2010. In his Letter proclaiming the Year for Priests, dated 16th June 2009, the Holy Father said that its purpose was to deepen the commitment of all priests to interior renewal for the sake of a more forceful and incisive witness to the Gospel. While praising the generosity and sacrifice of so many holy priests around the world, the Pope also acknowledged the infidelity of some, but then rejoiced in "the splendid example of generous pastors, religious afire with love for God and for souls". He encouraged his brother priests to learn from the example of the Curé of Ars: the witness of his life, his love for the Cross, his devotion to the Blessed Eucharist and the Sacrament of Penance, with the effect all this had on his parishioners. "In today's world, as in the troubled times of the Curé of Ars, the lives and actions of priests need to be distinguished by a forceful witness to the Gospel." The world needs priests to be holy and prayerful, he said. He particularly underlined a saying of the Curé of Ars: "The priesthood is the love of the Heart of Jesus."

Caritas in Veritate – Charity in Truth: third encyclical

The Pope's third encyclical, *Caritas in Veritate* ("Charity in Truth") was published on 29th June 2009. The title is inspired by St Paul's exhortation to practise "truth in charity" (Ephesians 4:15).

Nearly twice as long as the first two encyclicals, and addressed to "all people of good will", this was a densely-argued and penetrating study of "integral human development in charity and truth". The Holy Father set out the social teaching of the Catholic Church as it has grown and developed over the last century, and explained how it applies to the world of today. He showed that Christians cannot shirk their responsibility for practising charity in the light of the truth about man, the world, and the Creator. Once again, he pointed out that reliance on technology alone to solve the world's problems is doomed to end in failure.

Love essential to heal modern ills

The encyclical appeared at a time of serious economic problems worldwide. Its strength can be seen in various fields. On the one hand it was a response full of hope and practical possibilities, provided that its full message was taken on board. On the other hand, because it came as a specific response, at a specific moment in time, to the failure of the economy and development globally, it was able to show why they had failed. They failed, the Pope said, because of the absence of ethics and moral behaviour, so that truth was relativized, justice was not linked to charity, and the meaning of the common good was watered down. The Pope wrote, "As society becomes ever more globalized, it makes us neighbours but does not make us brothers." Human reason can understand and practise equality, "but it cannot establish fraternity" (no. 19). The overall answer to the failures seen in society is to be found in charity. "Only in charity, illumined by the light of reason and faith, is it possible to pursue development goals that possess a more humane and humanizing value. The sharing of goods and resources from which authentic development proceeds is not guaranteed by merely technical progress and relationships of utility, but by the potential of love that overcomes evil with good" (no. 9).

Rediscovery of fundamental values

In acknowledging the crisis the Holy Father used it to "rediscover fundamental values" in order to move forward. The current situation provided an occasion to re-examine these fundamental values and thus "to shape a new vision for the future", and to examine existing problems with charity in truth – to approach them "with confidence rather than resignation" (no. 21).

In his sweeping overview of society in the present economic and financial climate, Pope Benedict XVI showed how the absence of charity in truth played a significant part in the disastrous financial and social situation. He offered a new vision in all the areas he reviewed, making Christians see clearly that the future depends on them: "Only if we are aware of our calling, as individuals and as a community, to be part of God's family as his sons and daughters, will we be able to generate a new vision and muster new energy in the service of a truly integral humanism. The greatest service to development, then, is a Christian humanism that enkindles charity and takes its lead from truth, accepting both as a lasting gift from God" (no. 78). The Pope concluded with a specific call to the prayer of Christian faith: "Development needs Christians with their arms raised towards God in prayer" (no. 79).

Cardinal John Henry Newman

On 3rd July 2009 the Pope issued a decree recognizing a miracle attributed to the intercession of

Cardinal John Henry Newman. This meant that it was possible to proceed to his beatification, which had long been hoped and prayed for. It was confidently predicted that the Pope himself, who always had a great appreciation and love for Newman and his writings, would perform the beatification during his long-awaited visit to Britain in autumn 2010.

Czech Republic – and the heart of Europe

In September 2009 Pope Benedict spent two days, 26th-28th, in the Czech Republic. In that short time he spoke to many different groups. Outlining his purpose for the visit and acknowledging that the Catholic Church was a minority in this country at the "heart of Europe", he said that "usually it is creative minorities that determine the future". This upbeat message was characteristic of the whole trip. As always, he met civil authorities and cultural representatives and the leaders of the Catholic Church in the country.

Personal Ordinariates for convert Anglicans

Many requests were received from Anglican clergy around the world, desiring to enter into full communion with the Catholic Church. The Pope saw this as the work of the Holy Spirit. In the Apostolic Constitution *Anglicanorum Coetibus* dated 4th

November 2009, he wrote, quoting *Lumen Gentium*, that "the single Church of Christ, which we profess in the Creed as one, holy, catholic and apostolic, 'subsists in the Catholic Church, which is governed by the successor of Peter and by the Bishops in communion with him. Nevertheless, many elements of sanctification and of truth are found outside her visible confines. Since these are gifts properly belonging to the Church of Christ, they are forces impelling towards Catholic unity'."

This Apostolic Constitution opened the possibility of groups of Anglicans entering the Roman Catholic Church while still retaining their distinctive traditions and forms of worship. They would be able to form or join "Personal ordinariates", and the document explained how these would be constituted and organized. The Pope took this step because he understood how much such people valued their heritage and identity, and wanted to remove any unnecessary obstacles from their path towards the fullness of the faith. It was left open to the various groups of Anglicans around the world to respond in their own time to this possibility: the first to announce their intention to do so were some belonging to the group known as "Forward in Faith Australia", in February 2010.

Pope Pius XII and Pope John Paul II

On 19th December 2009 Pope Benedict issued a decree recognizing that Pope Pius XII and Pope John Paul II had practised the Christian virtues heroically, and that therefore they were declared "Venerable" by the Church. This means that in each case, after a miracle worked through their intercession has been recognized as authentic, they may be beatified. Even at the time of the funeral of John Paul II, there were appeals on the part of the public for him to be proclaimed a saint without delay, and Pope Benedict dispensed with the normal waiting-period of five years before the process of his beatification could begin.

In a homily he gave on 9th October 2008, the fiftieth anniversary of Pope Pius XII's death, Pope Benedict had said, "it is good to remember that holiness was his ideal, an ideal that he did not fail to propose to all. It was for this reason that he promoted the causes of Beatification and Canonization of people who belonged to different nations, people from all the states of life, roles and professions and allowed ample room for women. As a sign of steadfast hope, he held up to humanity Mary herself, the Woman of salvation, proclaiming the Dogma of the Assumption during the Holy Year of 1950." Referring to the ongoing controversy over Pope Pius XII's work for the Jews during World War II, Pope Benedict explained: "He often acted secretly and silently because, in the light of the practical situations of that complex period of history, he foresaw that only in this way could he avoid the worst and save the greatest possible number of Jews. Numerous and unanimous attestations of gratitude for his interventions were addressed to him at the end of the war, as well as at the time of his death, from the highest authorities of the Jewish world such as, for example, Israel's Minister for Foreign Affairs Golda Meir, who wrote: 'When fearful martyrdom came to our people, the voice of the Pope was raised for its victims. The life of our times was enriched by a voice speaking out about great moral truths above the tumult of daily conflict' and concluded with emotion: 'We mourn a great Servant of peace'."

Great saints and theologians

During 2009, after completing his series of audiences dedicated to St Paul and his Letters, the Holy Father continued with more of the great saints and theologians of Church, including Bede the Venerable, John Damascene, Cyril and Methodius, Anselm, Bernard of Clairvaux, and Peter Lombard.

7

Most intellectual of popes
Sixth year: 2010

In January 2010, at a ceremony in the Vatican, Pope Benedict was made an honorary citizen of Freising, Germany, where he studied as a seminarian. He was ordained a priest in Freising Cathedral on 29th June 1951.

Visiting the Rome Synagogue

On 17th January he visited Rome's Great Synagogue. He bowed his head in silence before the plaque commemorating the martyrdom of 1021 deported Roman Jews. In his speech, he paid homage to them: "How could one ever forget their faces, their names, their tears, the desperation faced by these men, women and children" rounded up as part of the "project of extermination of the people of the Covenant of Moses". He said, "The heartfelt prayer which Pope John Paul II offered at the Western Wall on 26 March 2000 comes back to my mind, and it calls forth a profound echo in our hearts: 'God of our

Fathers, you chose Abraham and his descendants to bring your Name to the nations: we are deeply saddened by the behaviour of those who in the course of history have caused these children of yours to suffer, and asking your forgiveness we wish to commit ourselves to genuine brotherhood with the people of the Covenant'."

Meeting the Bishops of England and Wales

From 24th January to 4th February, the Bishops of England and Wales travelled to Rome for their "*ad limina*" visit, as the diocesan Bishops of each country do every five years, to meet the Holy Father and discuss their diocesan ministry, and to make a pilgrimage "to the threshold" of the tombs of the Apostles Peter and Paul. In his address to them, the Pope referred to recently proposed legislation in the UK, some provisions of which could have the effect of forcing Catholic schools and other institutions to employ people whose beliefs and lives were in direct contradiction with the teaching of the Church. He said:

> Your country is well known for its firm commitment to equality of opportunity for all members of society. Yet as you have rightly pointed out, the effect of some of the legislation designed to achieve this goal has been to impose unjust limitations on the freedom of religious

communities to act in accordance with their beliefs. In some respects it actually violates the natural law upon which the equality of all human beings is grounded and by which it is guaranteed. I urge you as Pastors to ensure that the Church's moral teaching be always presented in its entirety and convincingly defended. Fidelity to the Gospel in no way restricts the freedom of others – on the contrary, it serves their freedom by offering them the truth. Continue to insist upon your right to participate in national debate through respectful dialogue with other elements in society. In doing so, you are not only maintaining longstanding British traditions of freedom of expression and honest exchange of opinion, but you are actually giving voice to the convictions of many people who lack the means to express them: when so many of the population claim to be Christian, how could anyone dispute the Gospel's right to be heard?

Lay apostolate

The Bishops of Scotland made their "*ad limina*" visit from 3rd to 10th February. After speaking to them about the Year for Priests, which included the 400th anniversary of the priestly ordination of the great Scottish martyr St John Ogilvie, the Holy Father told them,

> Hand in hand with a proper appreciation of the priest's role is a correct understanding of the specific vocation of the laity. Sometimes a tendency to confuse lay apostolate with lay ministry has led to an inward-looking concept of their ecclesial role. Yet the Second Vatican Council's vision is that wherever the lay faithful live out their baptismal vocation – in the family, at home, at work – they are actively participating in the Church's mission to sanctify the world.

The Church in Ireland

Four Irish Bishops travelled to Rome to meet the Pope over two days in February 2010 to discuss the tragic and shameful question of the sexual abuse of minors by Catholic priests, and the way this matter had been handled by the Irish hierarchy. According to the official statement published by the Holy See after the meeting,

> For his part, the Holy Father observed that the sexual abuse of children and young people is not only a heinous crime, but also a grave sin which offends God and wounds the dignity of

the human person created in his image. While realizing that the current painful situation will not be resolved quickly, he challenged the Bishops to address the problems of the past with determination and resolve, and to face the present crisis with honesty and courage.

He also expressed the hope that the present meeting would help to unify the Bishops and enable them to speak with one voice in identifying concrete steps aimed at bringing healing to those who had been abused, encouraging a renewal of faith in Christ and restoring the Church's spiritual and moral credibility.

The Holy Father also pointed to the more general crisis of faith affecting the Church and he linked that to the lack of respect for the human person and how the weakening of faith has been a significant contributing factor in the phenomenon of the sexual abuse of minors. He stressed the need for a deeper theological reflection on the whole issue, and called for an improved human, spiritual, academic and pastoral preparation both of candidates for the priesthood and religious life and of those already ordained and professed.

First Australian saint

On 19th February the Holy Father announced the forthcoming canonization of the Australian Sister Mary MacKillop (1842-1909), as well as of other holy men and women. Mary MacKillop, foundress of the Josephite order, would thus be the first Australian saint.

Footsteps of St Paul – visiting Malta

To continue his personal journey in the footsteps of St Paul, Pope Benedict announced that he would visit Malta, where St Paul was shipwrecked (*Acts* chapters 27-28), on 17th and 18th April 2010. The plan for the journey included a visit to the Cave of Saint Paul, and a meeting with young people.

Entrusting all to the Lord

The Australian theologian Tracey Rowland, in her book *Ratzinger's Faith: The Theology of Pope Benedict XVI,* speaks of the Holy Father as "one of the most intellectual Popes in history." She links his approach to Cardinal Newman's motto *Cor ad cor loquitur* ("heart speaks to heart"). Benedict XVI's deep theological knowledge has taught him that Christianity is above all a matter of the heart. The Pope is a Biblical theologian of world-wide renown, and he is "in love with the Church which for him really is the mystical bride of Christ."

His dedicated work for the Church during his first five years as Pope bears out the words he wrote in *Deus Caritas Est* in the year of his election. "In all humility we will do what we can, and in all humility we will entrust the rest to the Lord. It is God who governs the world, not we. We offer him our service only to the extent that we can, and for as long as he grants us the strength."

Bibliography

Benedict XVI, *Deus Caritas Est*, Catholic Truth Society, 2006
- *Spe Salvi*, Catholic Truth Society, 2007
- *Summorum Pontificum*, Catholic Truth Society, 2007
- *Caritas in Veritate: On Integral Human Development in Charity and Truth*, Catholic Truth Society, 2009

Joseph Ratzinger (Benedict XVI), *Jesus of Nazareth*, Bloomsbury, 2007

Scott Hahn, *Covenant and Communion: the Biblical Theology of Pope Benedict XVI*, Baker Brazos Press, 2009

Second Vatican Council, *Nostra Aetate: Declaration on the Relation of the Church to non-Christian Religions*, 28 October 1965

Aidan Nichols, *The Theology of Joseph Ratzinger: An Introductory Study*, T & T Clark Ltd, 1988

Tracey Rowland, *Ratzinger's Faith: The Theology of Pope Benedict XVI*, Oxford University Press, 2008

Francis Xavier Nguyen Van Thuan, *Prayers of Hope, Words of Courage*, Pauline Books & Media, 2002

Websites

www.vatican.va
www.ratzingerfanclub.com/
popebenedictxvinews.blogspot.com/
www.zenit.org

A world of Catholic reading at your fingertips ...

CTS

... now online
Browse 500 titles at

www.cts-online.org.uk

Catholic Faith, Life, and Truth for all